200 Animals

THE ULTIMATE

Animals Coloring Book

Is A Animals Stress Relieving Coloring Book, Disegned For Adults Relaxation.

200 Animals

Jack Daniel Raymond

THIS BOOK
BELONGS TO

____

____

____

color test page

Thanks For Your Feedback About Our Content On Advance,
We Are Getting Better And Better because of your Kindness and initiative.
Help Us Improve Quality of Content

Copyright 2020, Jack Daniel Raymond

CAPRICORN

ARIES

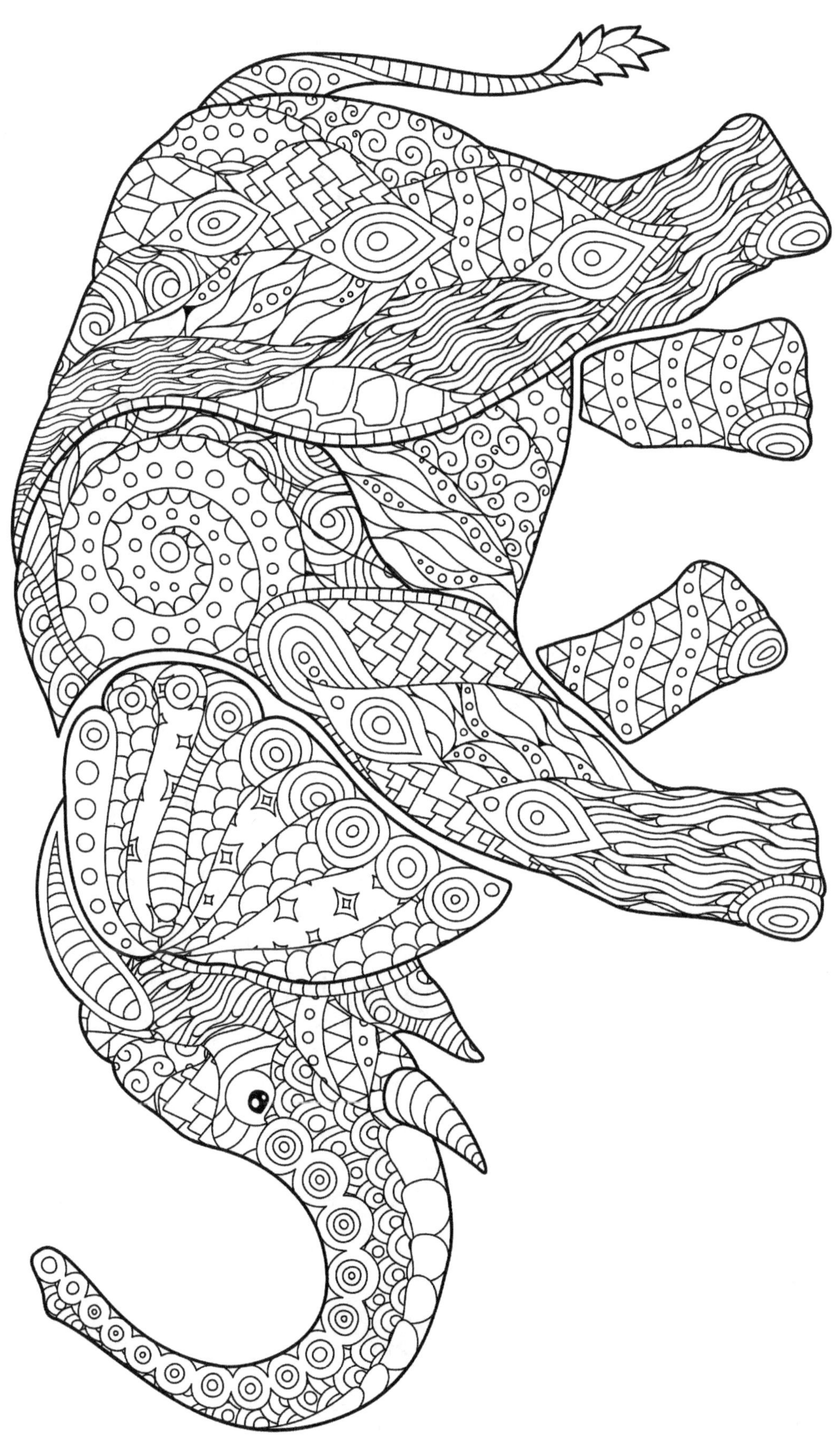

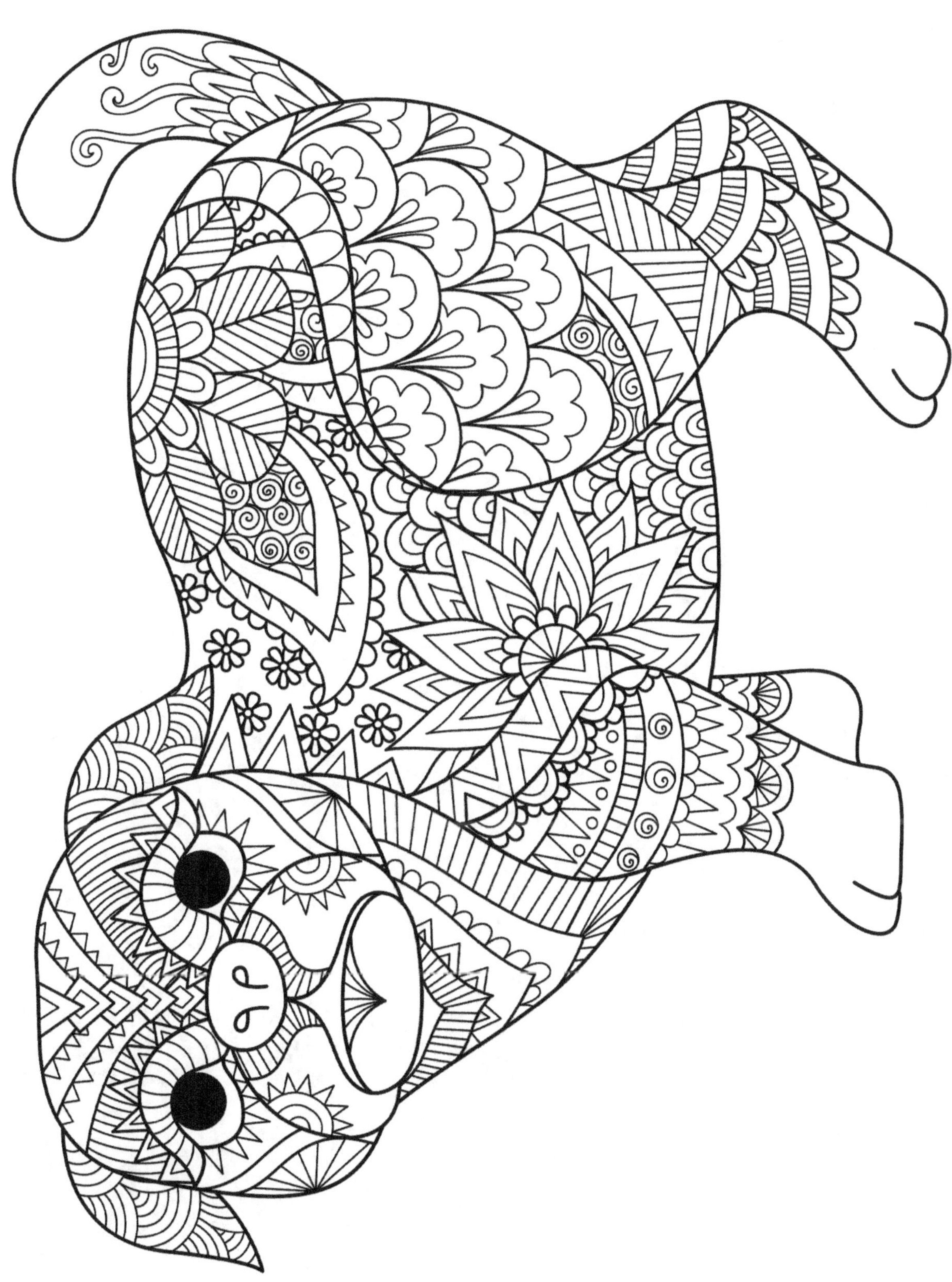

CANCER

SCORPIO

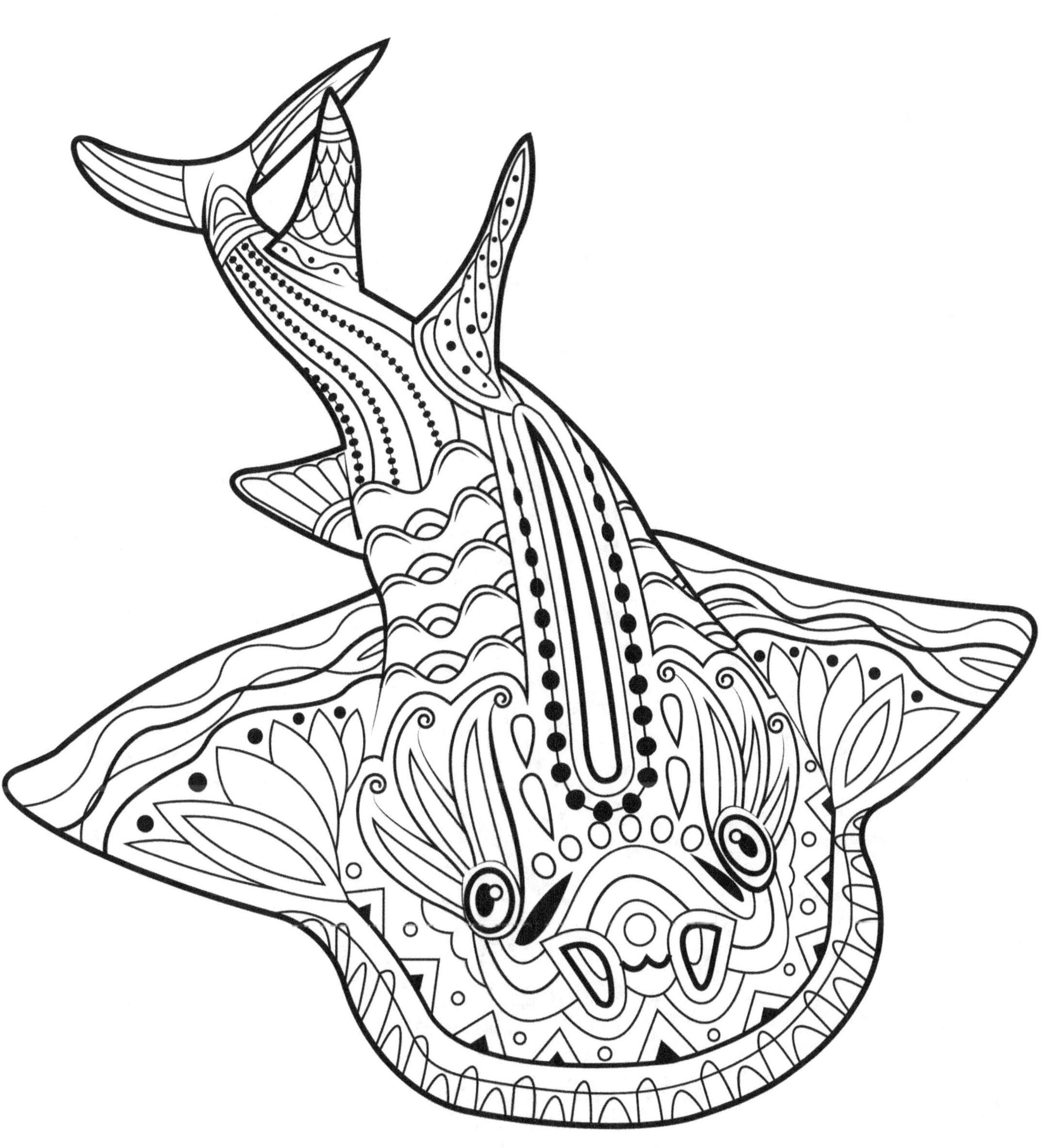

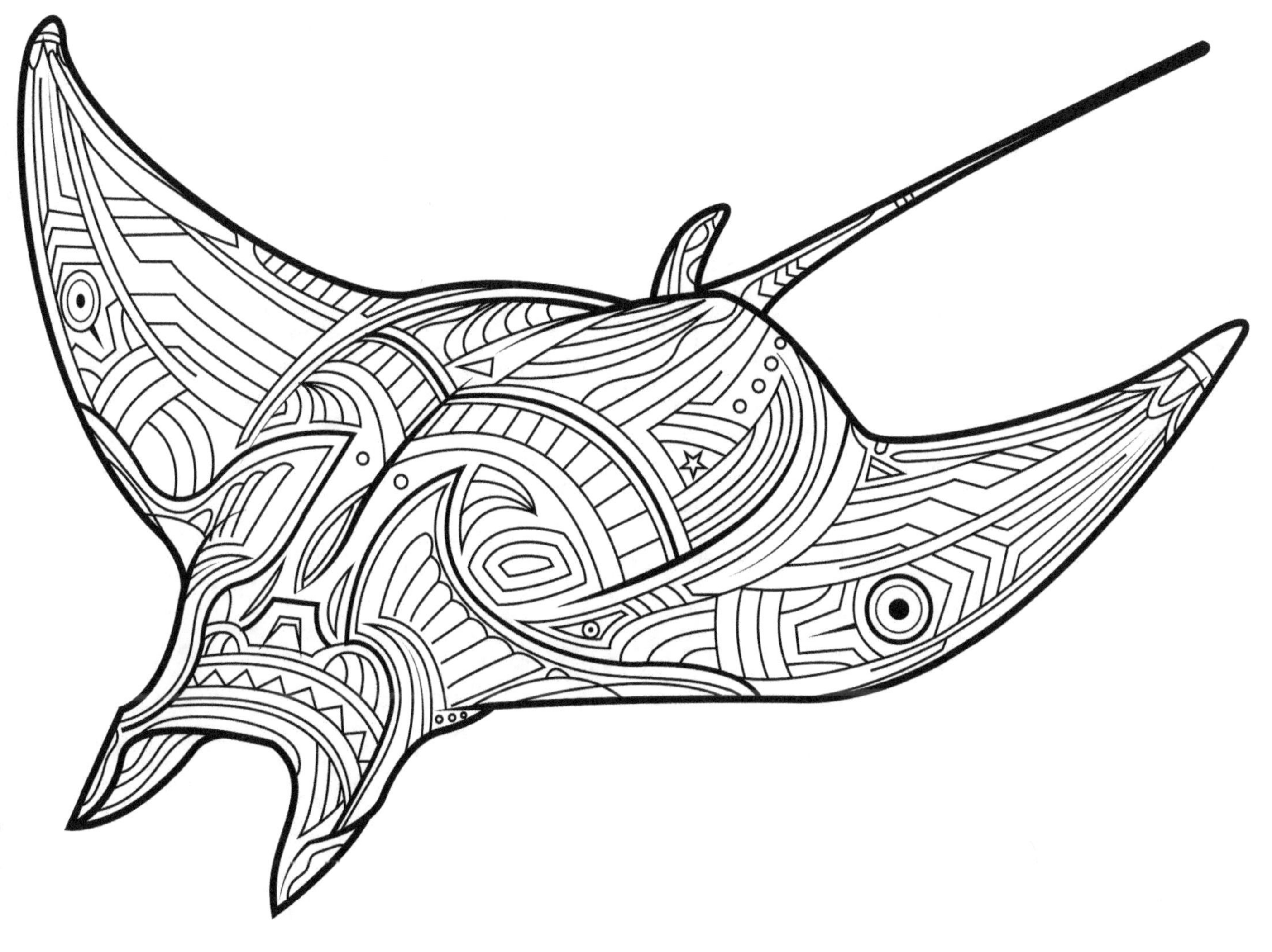

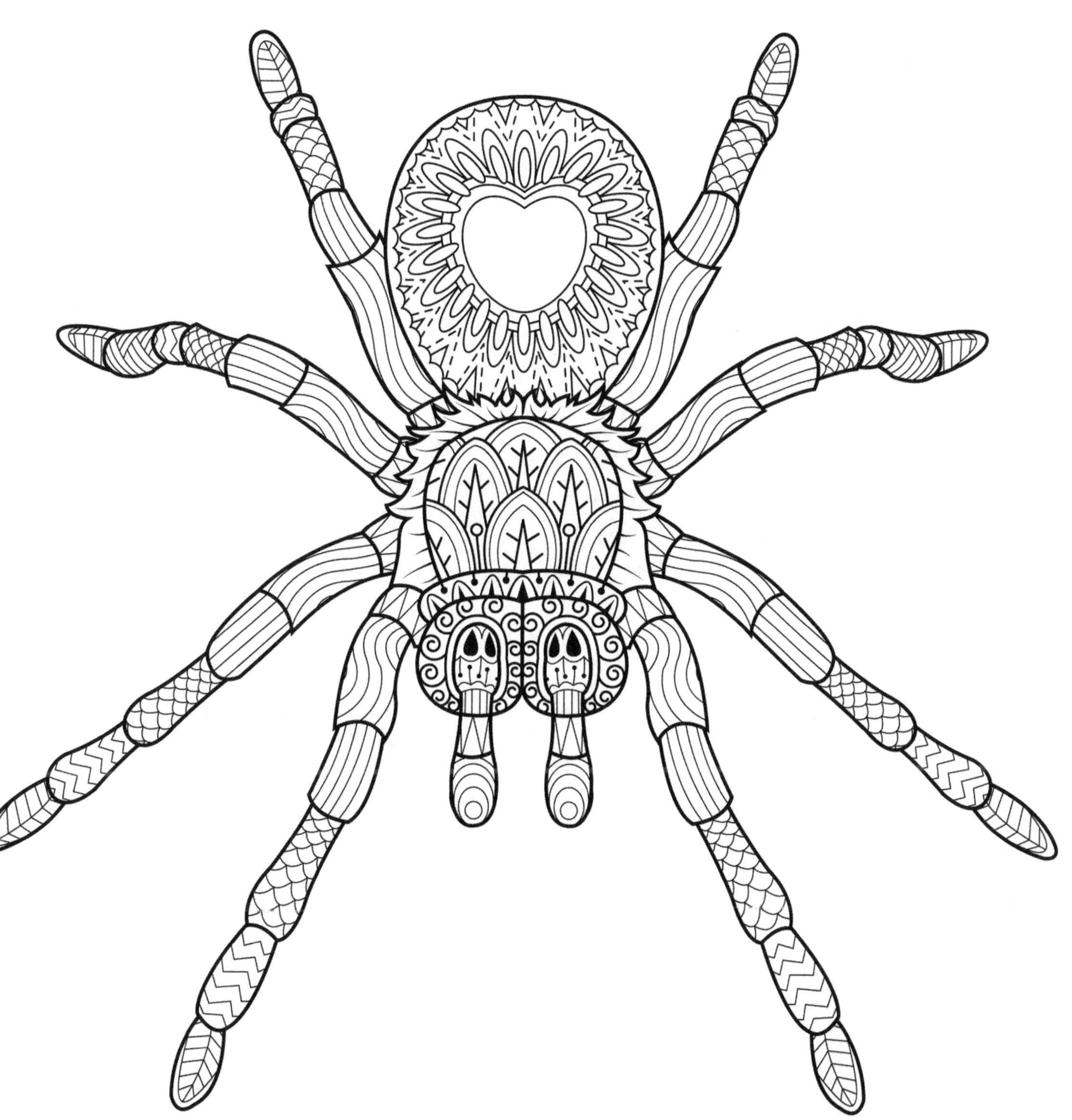

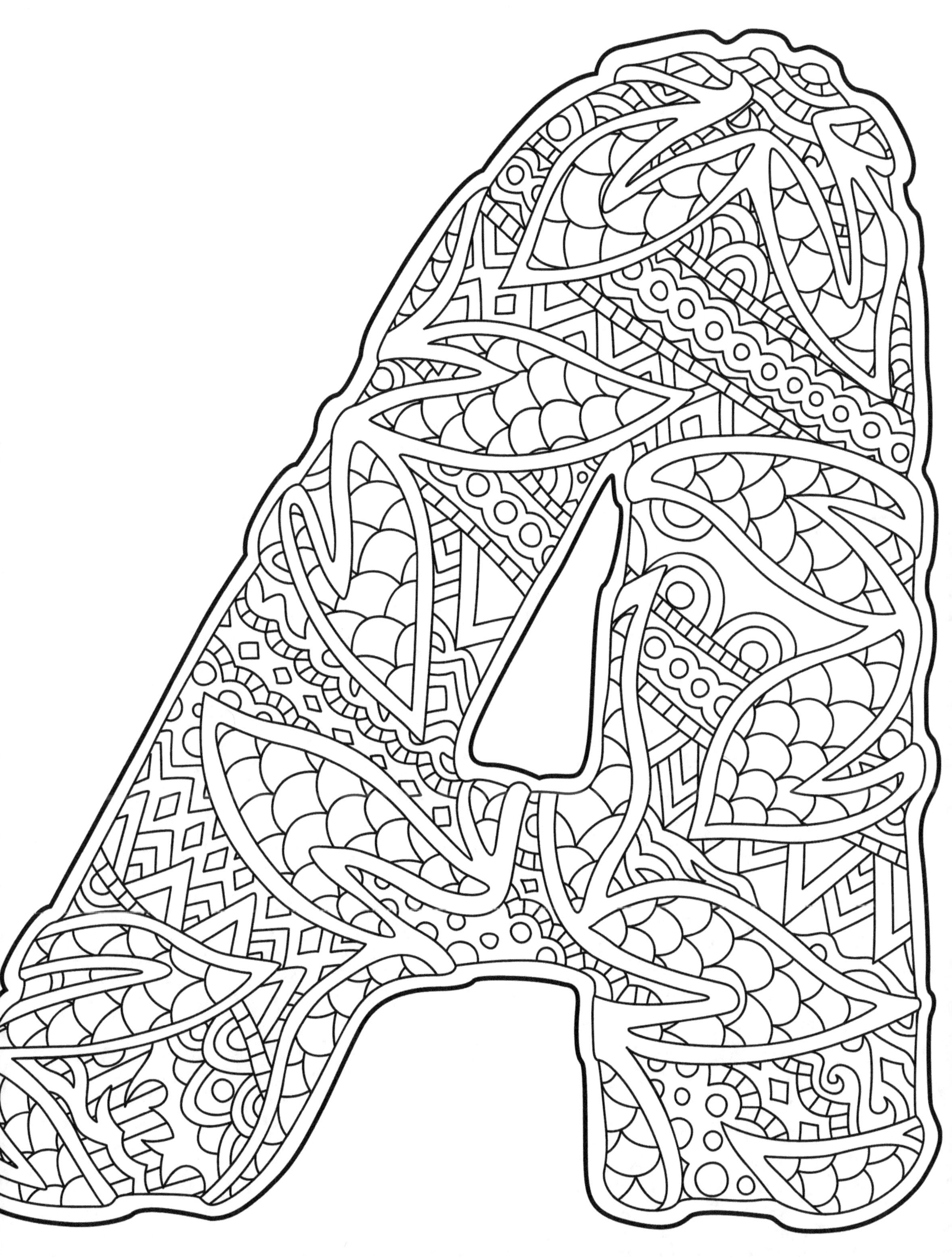

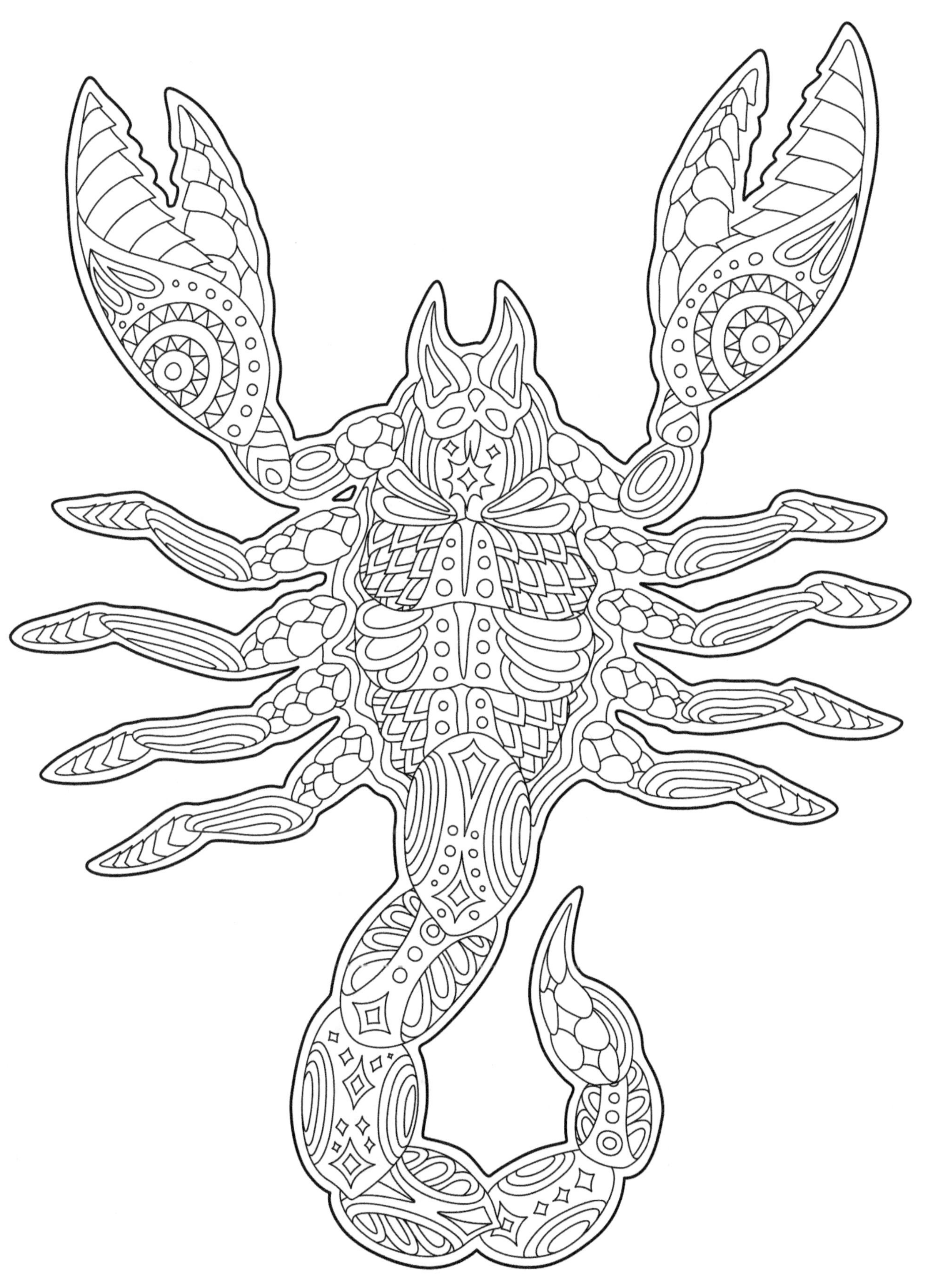